An Epistle on Judgment

Titles in the Series
Letters to the Devoted Follower of Christ

(in the order in which they were written)

AN EPISTLE TO THE MISERABLE
AN EPISTLE TO THE MODERATELY MISERABLE
AN EPISTLE ON JUDGMENT

An Epistle

on Judgment

By

A Little Anchor of the Church

Scriptures quoted from the King James Version (KJV) of the Bible. Please note that pronouns referring to God have been capitalized, though they are not in the KJV Bible.

The Little Anchor logo is derived from an image in the public domain and it and the name Little Anchor Books have no association with any other publishing company, nor was it intended they do so. By request, this volume has been self-published.

ISBN-13: 979-8-3304-2159-6

An Epistle on Judgment

MY dear friend in Christ, grace to you from God our Father and our Lord Jesus Christ, the One and Only Son of God.

I have heard that you have many questions regarding the subject of God's judgment and that the statements others are making lightly regarding judgment disturb your soul. I feel for you, for it is a heavy subject.

Questions regarding it can burden the soul until some degree of resolution is achieved. Here are some things I have learned about God and His ways. I apologize for the length of the letter, but I was concerned I might be misunderstood if I did not take care to clarify my meaning for this most crucial of subjects. I hope these thoughts are of some value to you. Perhaps they will at least begin to guide your meditations so that you may be enabled to receive greater illumination through whatever means of Truth God may send you.

Firstly, I pray in Jesus' Name that your soul may be enabled to receive the peace of God which passeth all understanding. So whether you feel at the end of this letter you possess helpful understanding, may you possess just the same the peace of God which extends beyond whatever degree of understanding you might obtain.

Secondly, though the matter of God's judgment is so pertinent in these days, strive to let not your soul remain unsettled for any length of time. Set aside confusion and thank God for the clarity of mind He has promised us in His Word.*

But I tell you at the very start, it is God who has purview in this matter, and no degree of understanding or confusion on your part will alter the manner in which He works out His judgment. There are soon going to be many events that initially we may not clearly understand, and we will have to choose either to simply trust or to be frustratingly confounded as we observe God's judgment come to this earth. Many warnings have been issued, and we have to trust that God has labored to reach those who have set themselves against Him (as well as those who have defied all attempts to awaken to what

---

* II Timothy 1:7—"For God hath not given us the spirit of fear; but of power, and of love, and of a sound mind."

He is doing in this earth). Remember that He has covenanted Himself to be our salvation, and so nothing He could do has been left undone. If at that time you feel you were not prepared enough, the fault is not in God, who is ever faithful to His promise to be the Light unto our path, as the psalmist wrote.* For a time, this may have to be enough comfort for the soul. Our prayers change things much, but in the end, HE WILL BE WHAT HE WILL BE.†

It has been on my heart to share with you a very simple distinction between those who fall under God's judgment and those who are exempt from it:

---

* Psalm 119:105

† Exodus 3:14—"And God said unto Moses, I AM THAT I AM: and He said, Thus shalt thou say unto the children of Israel, I AM hath sent me unto you." The KJV margin note for I AM THAT I AM provides an alternate rendering of "I save in the manner in which I save," and other versions also provide the alternate translation of I WILL BE WHAT I WILL BE. The sense that God will be and act independently according to the truth of His nature is consistent in all translations.

Those who fall under the purview of God's judgment are those who are unrepentant for their sins. This is the simple black-and-white distinction.

They are those who do not even consider their wrongful acts as violations of God's laws for themselves, and who persist in their ways despite cautionary words. Or they are those who have so stubbornly refused to leave off some idolatrous practice (such as ancestral worship*) that to awaken them to a higher authority God had no further recourse than to institute some judgment, the power of which went so far beyond the entities revered that

---

* Ancestral worship is an erroneous form of relationship between the earthly and the spiritual because it treats the spirits of mere men and women as though they have been able to raise themselves to a higher plane of existence by their own virtue. And if these can be worshipped, then there is no need for an atoning sacrifice. Those who have found eternal peace have done so because of God's grace to them; so it is to God worship is rightly rendered. And whether we understand something fully, some things are to be left off simply because God has told us they are wrong (e.g., witchcraft). If we really trust Him and His Word, we will obey His commands.

those souls had to reconsider the believed truth of their personal deities.

There are of course grey areas in personal application, which involve questions such as, Does this soul realize it lacks the spirit of repentance when it contemplates God? And, Does this make any difference to God? That is, Does He factor this into His equation for whether or not this soul must appear in His Court of Judgment?

I will give you the difficult truth immediately: a soul is not exempt from God's judgment without the repentance that acknowledges a need for a Mediator between God and Man. This is because the repentant soul full of fear of the LORD God Almighty — or just of a Most High God — cannot see how it can stand in the presence of God and live. It envisions Someone bearing the name Superhero coming to help it. It may not have the right name or have heard of the name JESUS. This God can work with (or so I sincerely believe) as long as the soul acknowledges there is one God above all and that it owes its existence to Him and recognizes it continues to exist due to His mercy. This soul will have to come face to face with the Saviour before it is permitted into Heaven, because it must choose to accept His Lordship over it if it is to live eternally in God's Home, for God made this Jesus to be Lord over us.* But God can communicate with such a soul, whereas He cannot with the one who has seared its conscience against Him. It is a complex matter, one which there is not time to discuss in depth in this letter.

Many Christians do not want to believe that God will allow to be kept from Heaven those who are of other tribes and cultures who are sincere persons with a conscience; and frankly,

---

* Acts 2:36—"Therefore let all the house of Israel know assuredly, that God hath made that same Jesus, whom ye have crucified, both Lord and Christ." And spiritually we enter into the same house of God to which Israel belongs.

there is no completely satisfying answer to this most difficult of human questions. The bottom line is that God will not allow into His children's heavenly Home any who cannot accept the reality of who He is and how He set the parameters of life for what He created. He will keep their Home safe for them at all costs. Each soul must work out these things itself while in a posture of proper fear of the One who has power over the life of the body *and* the soul.*

I tell you the truth, there *is* a need for a Mediator, and the soul with a sensitive conscience knows this. Any who declares otherwise does not understand the Consuming Essence of God.†

---

* See Philippians 2:12—"Wherefore, my beloved, as ye have always obeyed, not as in my presence only, but now much more in my absence, work out your own salvation with fear and trembling." And Matthew 10:28—"And fear not them which kill the body, but are not able to kill the soul: but rather fear Him which is able to destroy both soul and body in hell."
† Hebrews 12:28-29—"Wherefore we receiving a kingdom which cannot be moved, let us have grace, whereby we may serve God acceptably with

God does not shift into any particular state on account of us. Whatever He is in His Essence, He is at all times; this Essence is His natural state. So to believe God uses fire or fury as a weapon against a soul who goes against His ways is not to understand how He exists apart from any evil Man has done. He IS Consuming Fire because this is what He has forever been — the Fire consumes because It purifies whatever It touches. This is Its nature. It can no more help purifying what It touches than we can help breathing when we are not thinking about it. We do not breathe to commit harm toward others; it is a part of what we are physically; we are creatures who breathe air. Likewise, we do not feel convicted by our sin because God wants us always feeling remorseful; we feel convicted because when His Spirit touches us that Spirit is in Its nature

---

reverence and godly fear: for our God is a consuming fire."

Consuming Fire. He Will Be What He Will Be is His Name. It is our choice to receive Him or not as He is. It pleases Him enormously when we welcome Him without putting constraints on how He expresses Himself; and how He expresses Himself is always based on what He is in His Essence.

It is Man who cannot exist with God while in an adulterated state, because any adulteration corrupts the integrity of the soul's mettle. It cannot then withstand any test of its tensile strength without breaking.* And God's intent is not to have us be turned away upon facing the Gate to eternal life,† but for us to live forever without pain, loss, and death. That souls tainted by sin are not of a mettle to concurrently exist with God in His natural state is not His fault; it is theirs. No, they cannot fix this

---

* C. S. Lewis' novel *The Great Divorce* helps illustrate this concept if you are inclined to consider it.
† John 10:9—"I am the door: by Me if any man enter in, he shall be saved..."

themselves. But God provided the Way to buy back the spirit sin stole away. All He asks is that the soul acknowledge the Way He has chosen, which is Jesus Christ our Lord.

Repentance, the spirit of it or the act of it, does not save. It is the spirit of it which gives the soul opportunity to link itself to God's laws for the governing of Man's existence. When it sees its choice — to recognize that its guilt was its own (because true repentance does not shift the blame for its own sin onto another) — it humbles itself before God, admits its wrong, and submits itself to whatever recourse He has established for rectifying the wrongdoing.* Then in this submission

---

* Or the *wrongbeing*—we are all born into the state of being that father Adam passed onto his children so long ago. We repent for this state, freely acknowledging that we believe in our heart we would have succumbed to the same temptation he and mother Eve did since he had us in him at the time, regardless that we may strive to walk without committing wrongs (i.e., *wrongdoing*). Consider the principle taught us in Hebrews 7:10

the soul receives the Mediator without question. God essentially has said, "This is My Law: this is the Way to forgiveness, atonement, and reconciliation. Walk in It, which is even Jesus My Son." So the soul takes that Path because it wants to live.

This is the frank truth as I have come to understand it: the soul which cannot let go of its preferences—e.g., such as the desire to surround itself with icons of death and the occult—does not yet love life. For whatever reason—such as embracing those things because this soul is so fearful of death, believing they will desensitize it to death's horrors—these souls are still separated from God. I am not saying they would not gain Heaven. I am only saying that these things do most certainly interfere with the degree of relationship we can gain with God. For God will not overburden them even with His Life if

---

regarding this. I found Watchman Nee's book *The Normal Christian Life* to be helpful in comprehending this concept.

this is not what they do not yet desire (or they do not desire It above the other things), but this unquenchable, death-defying Life *is* His Essence. It would be like you pretending you are something other than you are simply to please another because you know he does not like the type of person you really are. Under such circumstances, how close can you really become? God will not pretend to be something other than what He is because you wish Him to be so. Instead He will keep His distance until you invite Him closer.

This is the true repentance that makes the rough way level* on the rocky

---

* See Isaiah 40:3-4 (which John the Baptist was referring to in John 1:23)—"The voice of him that crieth in the wilderness, Prepare ye the way of the LORD, make straight in the desert a highway for our God. Every valley shall be exalted, and every mountain and hill shall be made low: and the crooked shall be made straight, and the rough places plain." And Hebrews 12:13 teaches us to "make straight paths for your feet, lest that which is lame be turned out of the way; but let it rather be healed"—inferring that we need to be walking in the Way of God for us if we do not want to lose the path. It is the spiritually lame that lose their way.

road called Self-to-Spirit—that embracing of God's Way, not ours. And to repeat, what is that Way? That Way of our salvation is Jesus Christ our Lord —our Messiah*, Saviour†, and Atoning Sacrifice, the Propitiation of Our Sins.‡

Of course all this requires the foundational acceptance of Scripture as the inerrant Word of God—that great Book which instructs us on matters of life and death and which is entitled to a higher reverence than any other book or teacher. Well, it does if one has the Book, as you do. If you cannot bring yourself to accept the Christian Bible as God's eternal and inerrant Word, then my counsel does you little good since it is rooted in this belief. This Book declares the LORD the God Most High,

---

* Matthew 16:16—"And Simon Peter answered and said, Thou art the Christ [the Greek term for the Hebrew *Messiah*], the Son of the living God."
† Matthew 1:21—"And she shall bring forth a son, and thou shalt call His name JESUS: for He shall save His people from their sins."
‡ I John 4:10—"Herein is love, not that we loved God, but that He loved us, and sent His Son to be the propitiation for our sins."

the One alongside whom no other can stand remotely close (not even the devil). That we believe His authority does supersede all others is why we accept these truths as the final word on subjects, because this makes no other authority comparable to His. Each soul has to decide if it can receive this as a foundational truth. If it cannot, it will be tossed about on the waves of the sea of life as we are taught in Scripture.* If one day we accept God's Word on a matter, but on another day another word as definitive, then we are bouncing back and forth between truth and error (for if they are different words, they cannot both be true). God wills that we receive His Truth, but He will not force us not to accept words

---

* James 1:6-8—"But let him ask in faith, nothing wavering. For he that wavereth is like a wave of the sea driven with the wind and tossed. For let not that man think that he shall receive any thing of the Lord. A double minded man is unstable in all his ways." One of the purposes of anchorites is to keep those in their life-boat anchored to God's Truth.

that differ from His own. It is not His will that we be tossed back and forth on the seas of life; it is simply the natural result of not being anchored by the heavy weight of His Truth.* The living embodiment of this Truth was in Jesus of Nazareth, which is why He declared, "I am the way, the truth, and the life."†

In God's standard for Man's behavior, there is love and respect for one's fellows or there is just punishment for inflicting harm. And—this is important, so note this well—if one will not be judged under the new Law of Christ,

---

* There have been rumors—perhaps you have heard them—that many biblical books have been hidden from us but are soon to be revealed. This will certainly cause many persons of weaker faith to question the whole concept of scriptural inerrancy. I say that though some profitable words may have been censored by men in high places and their associated ungodly principalities, God saw to it that everything necessary to the revelation of Man's salvation was preserved for us across the centuries. If more is revealed, let us be faithful to test the spirit of it (I Thess. 5:21 and I John 4:1) and to receive whatever passes the test. But let us not allow ourselves to be tossed about by a few new reports as those who question the character of a Faithful Friend.

† John 14:6

one *has* to be judged under the old. There is not time here to explain why it is an either-or matter except to say that the soul who treats God as a relativistic Being, judging situationally rather than in principle and according to law, does not comprehend who He is or what He is about. It is good or evil, darkness or light, the old or the new.

Under the new, one is judged by whether or not Christ's Atoning Sacrifice can be applied to us. Have we received it as sinners who require a Saviour? If so, the Blood of Jesus has been applied, as the blood of lambs was applied to the Hebrews' doorposts in ancient Egypt.* If not, God has left us with no other option but to be judged under the old law, because He established creation upon the foundation of His divine Law. For the Law for Man was given *through* Moses; it already existed before him.† Remember that this

---

* Exodus 12
† John 1:17

Law did not apply only to the nation of Israel as Moses dealt with them in later days: consider the Flood in Noah's day, or the sentence the LORD pronounced over Cain for his sin of taking his brother's life. And no consequence was justified for Adam if no Law had existed by which his behavior could be judged. The general Law for Man's behavior was already in existence; Moses only recorded its contemporary application for a people who had been living and participating in an idolatrous culture for four centuries.

As in the new Law of Christ (that salvation is by Jesus alone), even under the old Law there was only one way to be right with God: the shedding of blood. Is it not written, "For the life of the flesh is in the blood: and I have given it to you upon the altar to make an atonement for your souls: for it is the blood that maketh an atonement for the soul"?* And since God loathed the

---

* Leviticus 17:11

shedding of blood by one neighbor to another,* we can understand better why He required animal sacrifice and abhorred human sacrifice.† There must be blood shed in the act of redeeming our soul from the kingdom of darkness back to the Kingdom of Light, from whence we were created. But Jesus' Blood is so powerful—in It is that purifying Essence of God—that His Sacrifice sustains its power forever.‡ Continual bloody sacrifice is an afront to the crucified Lamb of God, as though His Blood was insufficient to accom-

---

* See Genesis 4, wherein Cain slew his brother Abel, and the LORD said that "the voice of thy brother's blood crieth unto Me from the ground" (v. 10). Moreover, God told Moses to instruct the people after they came out of Egypt, "Thou shalt not kill" (Exodus 20:13).
† Human sacrifice demands that the sacrificer's life is of greater value than that of the one being sacrificed and that one person has the right to decide over another which is of greater value. Do you believe God looks at us from this perspective? If not, do we have the right to decide this about another?
‡ Hebrews 10:12, 14—"But this man, after He had offered one sacrifice for sins for ever, sat down on the right hand of God...For by one offering He hath perfected for ever them that are sanctified."

plish the task.* So if a soul will not receive this Blood, it must find recourse in some other blood according to the Law set forth for the governance of Man. For the life is in the blood.

It is the taking of the Life of God through Christ's Blood, or a soul must take the life of others to sustain its own, and this second way is never successful under God's Law because under the New Institution, Christ's Blood is the only sufficient Remedy. One blesses us with eternal life; the other curses us with only a half-life or half-death. Some who hate God discover the inverse of

---

* I am not saying however that God would not reinstitute the old sacrifices for a time—say, when the third temple is rebuilt in Jerusalem—if this is what it takes to link the illustration of the lambs necessary to atonement in the old covenant to the Lamb of God, Jesus of Nazareth, in the new one. Under the purpose of a clearer testimony of Christ, I do not believe such sacrifices would be an afront to God. They would be the acceptable sacrifice for the salvation of many souls if these souls came to an understanding of a Mediator by the living illustration of having to bring a spotless little lamb to the altar. It is the continual bloody sacrifice by those looking to another way of atonement and who set aside Christ's sufficient Sacrifice that is an affront to God.

this principle that the life is in the blood, and they use it to transfer the life-force of another to themselves for the gaining of power, wealth, and longer life. But most go to their grave without ever realizing the importance of the life being in the blood, and perhaps this is better (if these souls were reconciled to God), for the soul who makes use of this principle in its inverted state pays a heavy price, even eternal damnation if it does not see the error of its ways. Since the institution of the New Law, there is only one Blood that provides appeasement for the guilt of sin. Here is the Word of the Lord: "For it is not possible that the blood of bulls and of goats should take away sins."* This passage continues until it declares: "He taketh away the first, that He may establish the second."†

---

* Hebrews 10:4—or the blood of any animal, such as a human one.
† Hebrews 10:9

I say again, if a soul refuses to be judged under the New Law, wherein Christ's Blood is ever at work against sin-guilt, it must be judged under the old covenant, which the Word of God declares to be insufficient to supply atonement. This is the basis for condemnation—not that God would exclude but that souls refuse the Way of Salvation He has so graciously provided for them. He requires no work from a soul except that it believes the One He sent.*

These are no simple matters. Your soul was disturbed by its questions because these are weighty and honest questions about the ways of God. I pray that if what I write is truth, your soul will discern it and be enabled to receive it.

God will not cease to discipline His children as needed throughout their life on this earth. For we are instructed to

---

* John 6:29

remember, "My son, despise not thou the chastening of the Lord, nor faint when thou art rebuked of Him: for whom the Lord loveth He chasteneth, and scourgeth every son whom He receiveth. If ye endure chastening, God dealeth with you as with sons; for what son is he whom the father chasteneth not?"*

But judgment is the rendering of an official legal verdict. For those who have placed their confidence in the Blood of Jesus, all legalities have been satisfied forever by this one Sacrifice†; therefore there is no need to appear in the LORD's Court for His verdict regarding our fate. The scroll has already been marked by the Blood and sealed by the Holy Spirit.‡ God will, however, extend His hand into our life

---

* Hebrews 12:5-7, which is referring to the teaching of Proverbs 3:11-12.

† Hebrews 7:27—"Who needeth not daily, as those high priests, to offer up sacrifice, first for His own sins, and then for the people's: for this He did once, when He offered up Himself."

‡ Ephesians 1:13

as a loving father does for any erring child. So do not expect sins to escape chastisement. Some undergo this disciplining with the forfeit of their earthly life due to the severity of their sin, and it is not always clear why God resorts to such lengths to deal with that person's sin. You must choose for yourself whether you will trust His judgment at such times.

In the person whose soul is not completely seared against the flow of God's Spirit, repentance is still possible in order to have a place in Heaven. Do not conclude that someone went to hell because God's judgment was pronounced upon him and his life was demanded as a just sentence for his crimes. Tragically, some do end up in hell forever, but not all. To commit heinous crimes requires a hardening of the soul, a belief that one's own life is of greater value than the one being used, abused, and sacrificed; and continual acts of this kind will eventually sear the conscience. If it does not, if perhaps crimes were committed because fear for oneself or one's loved ones being threatened was powerful enough to compel it to this choice, I daresay noticeable signs of interior agony will be seen by those closest to them, and the truth will be revealed someday, for it is written, "Fear them not therefore; for there is nothing covered, that shall not be revealed; and hid, that shall not be known."[*]

Pray for heart-softening if you feel any compassion at all for those being judged—and I believe you must feel this since the matter of God's judgment has been so troublesome to you. Soul-softening is more vital to a soul's fate than whether it continues to live in this flesh. As for their victims, by and large they are with the Lord (and certainly every child sent to its death by those who have violated the Law are with Him). I believe they would not return

---

[*] Matthew 10:26

here if you asked them. They are happy above in the work they do for the Body of Christ and would not return to this body of death.*

The only exceptions to this law of repentance are for those who are incapable of such reasoning as is granted to a developed mind, but the rest of the soul—the will and the emotions—freely and wholeheartedly receives this Way of God. This is what occurs in children or in some of the simple-minded, those who suffer with severe developmental disabilities. They accept Jesus as Saviour and Lord because it is part of the truth of God's creation to them. With all the functionality of soul they possess, they acknowledge whatever God says is the truth. That they cannot reason in an advanced way does not detract from the truth of the matter that they adhere

-----

* Romans 7:24—[Paul was asking,] "O wretched man that I am! who shall deliver me from the body of this death?" or, "this body of death," is the margin translation.

to God's Way of Salvation for Man with all the fullness of soul they possess. And this is how God perceives it—that with all their soul has to give, even if the bulk of functionality is in their heart (being too young or undeveloped to do much else than to love), they give this soul to the One who loves them. Therefore they satisfy the demand God places on all souls that it should decide for itself the way it will go.* I am not trying to make it seem as if no grey areas exist—some souls are highly developed enough to experience anger at God for seemingly making them less than what the rest of us are. Pray for them, but also trust them to God, who is fully able to reach them too with His Holy Spirit. Again, do not be certain you know upon whom the LORD will pronounce judgment and on whom He will not.

---

* Joshua 24:15—"...choose you this day whom ye will serve."

God — the LORD, whose name is a reminder of His rightful authority over us — asks a tremendous amount of loyalty from those who profess to be His. He expects faithfulness and the exercising of a non-judgmental attitude toward Him during seasons of crisis. The younger the soul, the more lightly He deals with judgmentalism; but as the soul matures, He expects its attitude toward Him to mature as well. Have you ever felt ashamed as to how you once spoke with people when you were young and stupid? Would you speak in the same manner to them today as you did when barely of age? If not, doesn't God deserve as much respect?

Our unsettled state is fully understood by God when we have major life questions, such as when a loved one dies. He graciously answers such questions as time passes and as we give Him time to speak. And our revelation, I might add, is in proportion to how much truth the soul is able to receive on the subject of life and death.

It is another matter entirely however to judge God for the way groups of persons die—for example, those with cancer—or when waves of death occur, such as when millions died during World War I due to what was classified as a flu epidemic, or the way all the firstborn of the unprotected houses died in Egypt during the time of the plagues. In the first place, God is not responsible for the destructive machinations of evil men and their myriad wicked schemes, which is what the WWI flu appeared to be. Additionally, the soul begins to step onto a precarious ledge when it decides God is guilty of wrongdoing for not interceding to halt waves of deaths that take the lives of many innocents. And for one to decide that some of those such as Egypt's firstborn were innocent—or not guilty enough of any sin to warrant such a harsh fate—is also precarious footing.

And I repeat, any innocents and those reconciled to God are far happier in Heaven with God than they would be here on earth. Perhaps this will help you as you reconcile yourself to God's ways of dealing with Man. *They are not dead*: He brought them into *greater life*. We should not take their deaths lightly, for they were robbed of whatever God intended for their lives here on earth, and this earth was robbed of the blessing He intended them to be for Man here. Nevertheless, every blessing that Heaven contains has been given to them, and they are happy.

I must ask you—not to be harsh, but so that it is clear that each soul must inquire this of itself—who are you to judge God? Who are you to decide whether God's direct or permissive actions are right when you look across such large distances of time and space—or even just the long space to what is occurring in other parts of the world when you cannot see for yourself what is happening, and when it has been incontrovertibly demonstrated that news programs are narratives crafted to guide the thinking of the masses and not accurate reports of current events? I ask you most sincerely and without rancor—*who are you* to judge God?

The soul truly reconciled to God, who truly knows His character, will not respond in such a way when His strong, long arm of judgment manifests itself in this earth. He waits long years and whole eras keeping that arm restrained until sin reaches its full measure. Remember what was written of Abraham's covenantal encounter with the LORD: "And He said unto Abram, Know of a surety that thy seed shall be a stranger in a land that is not theirs, and shall serve them; and they shall afflict them four hundred years; and also that nation, whom they shall serve, will I judge: and afterward shall they come out with great substance.

And thou shalt go to thy fathers in peace; thou shalt be buried in a good old age. But in the fourth generation they shall come hither again: for the iniquity of the Amorites is not yet full."*

Consider how many truths are compacted in these few verses about how God works: one, He prepares the soul willing to hear about what is to come. Two, He does not lie about what is to come but tells the truth, though He chooses not to go into gritty detail regarding the hardships to come. Three, He is frank about the reality that He does indeed judge at times. Four, He does not fail to bless His own people even during times when they see His judgment rain down on those around them, or hear of it occurring in the future as a done thing as Abram did. Five, He is honest that there are those who will not live in their earthly tent to see the fulfillment of the blessing or the

---

* Genesis 15:13-16

judgment that has been ordained,* but states frankly that they are to go "in peace." That is, we are not to conclude that Abraham departed for some other place than Paradise simply because he did not live to see the fulfillment of God's word to him, which we seem to do for many souls simply by the circumstances in or the time at which they die. Six, He chooses not to enact His judgment until the bowls of Man's iniquity are full, which is His prerogative if He is indeed the highest Judge

---

* Regarding the judgment aspect, it is not ordained arbitrarily to happen, but ordained because of what Man chose of his own free will that God could see happening across time. God saw that the Amorites would not cease their bloody practices and that they would fill those bowls of iniquity someday, and He was choosing to defer transferring ownership of that land from them to Abram's descendants until those bowls were filled. This was just on God's part, and the Canaanite tribes who practiced all manner of idol worship and bloody rituals, had four *hundred* years to turn from their wicked ways. Yet they chose not to. Scripture is unspecific about what all those practices were (though it does reveal the sin of child sacrifice), but it does make it clear that God considered them worthy of judgment. We choose to trust or not that He is capable of deciding such matters justly.

on a bench. And seven, since He tells Abraham about waiting on the Amorite tribe until their sins shall reach a fullness, He is also giving Abraham a reason as to why he will not be living to see the fulfillment of His promise to his seed: His reason for waiting has nothing to do with how Abraham has lived before Him. He will not fulfill the promise within Abram's lifetime because this would require acting unjustly toward those who might still receive mercy. That He knows they will receive judgment instead is not enough cause for Him to dispense with a period of grace, during which they might choose to repent.

At the end of time, God Most High will emerge wholly unstained in His judgments. All creation will observe how every mercy and kindness were extended for as long as possible given all the factors. The hard truth many cannot accept is that yes, God will permit the murder of innocent children

He knows will come Home to Him while He endures a period of grace for the unrepentant. For He does not desire that they should spend eternity in hell; He desires that they repent and be reconciled to Him. And if you could ask those souls innocent of any crime worthy of being murdered, I believe they would tell you themselves that it is better that they died when they did than that those unrepentant souls did (say, because God struck them down before they could commit murder against an innocent) and went to hell because of an unrepentant state. God *will* avenge their deaths, however, so we must not take these matters lightly, regardless that these souls are presently happy with Him. Their blood will continue to cry out until the wrong done to them has been satisfied.* And the only

---

* An example of a group of innocents are those who are murdered because of their testimony for the Lord: Revelation 6:9-11—"And when He had opened the fifth seal, I saw under the altar the souls of them that were slain for the word of God, and for the testimony which they held: and they

satisfying response to God for these great crimes is the presentation on the heavenly altar of the Blood of Jesus Christ, the One made to be Saviour and Lord. This is why we must receive It, because there is nothing else that can be placed on that altar that God will consider in our defense.

Does this word to Abram satisfy you to some degree? Perhaps you had not seen in it all that God was trying to convey (and for certain there is more than I have said). Recall to yourself that God never judges prematurely or without waiting the full measure of time that any just system of law requires before interceding in a situation. God readily forgives those who repent of their sins or their judgment of Him.

---

cried with a loud voice, saying, How long, O Lord, holy and true, dost Thou not judge and avenge our blood on them that dwell on the earth? And white robes were given unto every one of them; and it was said unto them, that they should rest yet for a little season, until their fellowservants also and their brethren, that should be killed as they were, should be fulfilled." God forbears to act before a fullness of time and number has occurred.

The biggest hindrance to receiving this forgiveness is not God: it is that many souls do not believe they have done anything over which they need to repent.

And on the matter of repentance, if you cannot comprehend God's right to judge and the justness of His sentences, then you also cannot comprehend the excessive liberality He applies for those who have exercised true repentance for their sins. Moreover, it is by *His* standard of human behavior we repent, not ours. This is what makes our repentance sincere. Having violated *God's* sense of morality, we acknowledge our wrong of our own free will.

Many live their whole life as though God has no sense of morality, that as long as they can see no consequences on themselves or those around them, neither has God been offended by their immorality. But God is the purest of all entities — pure love, pure feeling, pure mercy, pure lovingkindness — pure in everything He feels, says, and does. If He acts with wrath but also with mercy, you can be sure that His wrath was not adulterated in any way, and His mercy was pure mercy, untainted by anything else. That they were operating in tandem is not something I can well explain at this time; but that anything in Him is a mixture in the sense that any attribute becomes less or other than it was in its pure state, is an erroneous belief. We cannot commit impure acts or live in impure states and still be reconciled in a practical way with One who is always pure. It is again something of corrupted mettle that believes it can abide the presence of a Mettle that cannot be consumed by anything, but Itself is a Consuming Fire.

The longer I live the more I am convinced that the natural human state since Adam's fall from grace is stupidity. If God is burdening your soul to reconcile matters such as these, it is because He is trying to relieve you of some of your natural stupidity, as He does for any soul willing to grow in Truth. Be grateful you feel something on this matter, for many walk about unburdened by any questions. They are content merely to eat, take their pleasure in various recreations, sleep, and then start the cycle all over again. God does not even occur to them on a daily basis, let alone continually throughout the day as He does for you. Though you feel unsettled and you worry that your questions mean you are somehow not right with God, I can tell you with confidence that your soul is in a much safer place than it is for them.

And because your soul is in this place where it seeks God's answers, I will be frank with you, praying you can receive what I am writing: the Church has entered an historical hour when many are going to be judged—not merely those of the world, but those *of the Body*. And many more may also die (please note I said *may*) because in their heart they do not want to be bothered about leaving Egypt, about what such a great journey would entail.* They do not want to set out on a long trek to move their whole life into a new land (and having to leave a great deal behind, even though these things are going to be unnecessary where they are going), as well as learning new laws and a whole new way of living, even though it is going to be a far better way of living than the one they would have left. They don't really care that they would have far greater freedom than they have ever known, especially be-cause until recently they did not think much about having been born into slavery. They feel that the quality of life they have had hasn't really been so bad; only in

---

* I myself knew a person who I believe passed into Heaven for this very reason, for she was aware of much of this and still chose to say, thinking of her own situation, "Some didn't leave Egypt." So instead of making her suffer a choice while her loved ones left Egypt—left lives of lack and debilitation—God the loving Father graciously brought her Home.

more recent years has it been a little difficult, they would admit. Yet Egypt—i.e., the synonym for the great world system of governance, economy, and so forth—will be decimated in this day just as it was in ancient days when the LORD intervened for the sake of His people.

The verdict: there is no going back to the relatively comfortable life once experienced there. Please understand: I am in no way saying life will be *un*comfortable where we are going. I am only saying that the comfort associated with the old familiar life we knew is falling away. But God never gives something new without it being better than the old. It is we who settle for less than He wants for us. As we stumble with fatigue into the first comfortable oasis we find, though it is only an ant-infested log in a marshy bog instead of a rock swept clean and warmed by the sun, we set ourselves down and proclaim we have reached our destination. Stupid.

What might happen to those who do not wish to move forward? They do not seem to understand that in post-plagues Egypt, the land was left barren and impoverished. They do not seem to understand that those leeks and melons will not be had after the LORD has left the world system devastated.* They would more readily perish of starvation and lack in Egypt, the world's system of provision, than they would

* Numbers 11:5—"We remember the fish, which we did eat in Egypt freely; the cucumbers, and the melons, and the leeks, and the onions, and the garlick." But these were apparently not available after the plagues left all the crops decimated. Exodus 10:15—"And there remained not any green thing in the trees, or in the herbs of the field, through all the land of Egypt." Even if available in Goshen, it was unrealistic of the people to believe their Egyptian overlords would not have just come to pillage from Goshen to meet their own needs. So these foods would not have been available to them even if they had returned or stayed in Egypt.

from what God has made ready for us beyond these boundaries of slavery.*

(I wish to add that I do not believe there is any lack of provisions for the people, though whether they are squirreled away somewhere or God provides supernaturally, I do not know. I suspect we will see both. It may be that the world system of distribution will be interrupted for a time. God has promised us that as Jehovah-Jireh He can provide for those who dare to declare, as Abraham did, that He will do so.† Let us believe Him on this.)

Would a loving Father leave His own to such a fate? Do you think it is remotely possible He will free them by bringing them to their heavenly promised land instead, since they just can't bring themselves to leave the only life they have known to reach an earthly promised land? –even if it is a life of

---

* Most of us are born into debt-slavery, for this is how the world's financial system works (and arguably, our governmental system as well).
† Genesis 22:14

slavery and the new life is one of freedom? Would a loving Father just leave them there to suffer perpetually, effectually saying, "Oh well, just suffer affliction all your days since you didn't want to come with us into a new country"?

And how are you going to respond? Are you going to lump these souls in with all those dying from the judgment that is a just sentence for the crimes they committed against humanity and for treason? If you do, then you really do not understand God, His character and His ways, at all. He wants you to understand Him and why He is doing what He is. He wants you to embrace a Kingdom ideology and to let go of the ideology of deprivation and survival we have known all our lives. There are going to be things you may be tempted to judge Him for because we have reached the point where to protect us, He must judge those who in their hearts want to destroy us. His decrees are at times going to appear harsh. You will have to decide if you can keep your faith in Him unwavering and confident. For His part He has done all He can to convince you by the words we have been given that His will is good and His intent is to bless, not harm. Yet not all will bring their soul into agreement with this.

And because you inquired of my opinion on the subject—if you do not yet understand—treason is subversion; it is betrayal against one's neighbors in order to assist an enemy to come in to defeat them, unto death if necessary. It is not a crime confined to one or two nations of a certain type of government. It is a crime applicable in any nation whose government declares there is one set of laws for all—i.e., that those in high places are not exempt from judgment simply because they occupied higher places than the masses. If there has been a betrayal of trust, there is a right to bring the charge.

God told us not to bear false witness against our neighbor or to covet what our neighbor has.* Do you believe it is doing right by one's neighbor by acting with duplicity toward their destruct-tion, especially because in doing so that person believed she would personally profit by this deception? And what of those who sincerely believe we would be better off under a strict socialist rule and who are (stupidly) laboring toward this end? What will God do with them if they cannot be convinced that as God has given human souls the privilege of choosing which way they will go, so ought we to permit of our neighbors? It will seem that some of those judged did not comprehend what they were doing or that they were committing crimes so very wrong (if indeed these useful idiots will be judged at all; I personally believe they ought to just take an oath of loyalty to the Republic and then give them time to awaken, but we will see

---

* Exodus 20:16-17

what those in authority decide to do; I am not saying that my opinion matters, just that I have one). Will you trust God to decide rightly, or will you judge Him for His legally binding decrees instead?

These are very serious matters to God. If He chooses to let someone live, let them live. If He chooses to require a heavy price from them, that is for Him to decide. Do you really want to preside as judge over their fate, even eternal fate in the cases of execution, or would you rather the LORD put on His robe and sat in His High Bench and decided on these matters?

And let us earnestly pray for those who must decide the fate of many. It is easy to say after plague, accident, or sickness that the LORD chose the fate of persons who died by these means. But what of executions? Let us pray now that what results from the justice being poured into this earth that all that happens is according to the LORD's standard of justice. Let there be mercy where there may be mercy; but if death is the just sentence that men with authority believe must be carried out, then pray for these who must bear in themselves these irrevocable decisions. And pray for the souls falling into the grave and trust that God did all He could and is doing all He can until the very last second to bring them Home to Him.

God's mercy and lovingkindness are everlasting.* His harsh judgment upon many all at once comes but once an eon, and most of what history records cannot rightly be attributed to His arm of judgment but to His permissive will as He waits to judge until bowls of iniquity are full. His protection over the wicked as He waits for the end is astounding, and His protection over the duly repentant is clearly far beyond what you have understood it to be. Sometimes it is just for a person to be put to death for his crimes, even if there

* So stated 26 times in just Psalm 136.

is repentance that leads to soul-transformation, and this not always because God cannot or wills not to grant a reprieve, but because the people — those masses of souls who stupidly did not strive to meditate on these matters when they had time (and I do count myself among them as one who has been stupid too) — need to see how serious a matter it is to violate the laws God set for the standard of Man's behavior. We tend to make too little of this standard as soon as a reprieve comes, whether we personally escaped some horrible fate by the skin of our teeth or someone infamous does whom we have idolized.

Christ's Blood washes clean of sin every soul who receives Jesus as the Atoning Sacrifice for sin. This is why we plead it, especially in times when great judgment is seen. The soul who has committed great sins is as clean and forgiven as the one who merely has the taint of inherited sin upon it but who is all but pure of sins of commission. The power of the Blood of Christ cannot be limited by sin or any degree of it, or Christ had no victory over sin at all.

Among the truly repentant, God can afford to show mercy because He knows the state of their soul has been transformed by His indwelling presence to make that person into one who never again wants to return to a lifestyle filled with wickedness. Don't you see? In permitting such a person to live and to be reintegrated into society, there is no risk of that person aligning himself again with death and destructtion. But is this what He will choose to do? You may find yourself tempted to judge God because He took someone you were convinced could be integrated into the human community once again, and you do not understand why He did not show more mercy. Well, perhaps mercy was not what that person wanted. Perhaps some persons have had enough of living with their sin and long for death as the one thing that might wash away some of the stain upon their soul. And so this is what God arranged for them. It may bring you more peace that they had lived, but the forfeiture of their life may have brought them more peace.

Be careful about what you decide about God, for we live in unprecedented days and He is through enduring us playing around regarding such matters. He is through letting things remain light matters that to Him are sober ones—throwing around the table statements of great consequence as though our opinions are something special when we had hardly given thought to what we declared. I am not saying how He will express His doneness with this; this is entirely up to Him. One soul may experience outward repercussions in his life for the looseness of his tongue, while another may only feel humbled by an inner conviction. He will deal with each of us as He will. Remember what our Lord told Peter shortly before His Ascension: "Jesus saith unto him, If I will that he tarry till I come, what is that to thee? follow thou Me."* Frankly, as the King of the universe He has the right to be done with our frivolous attitudes about sin and sentencing, especially since heinous crimes have been committed — and especially as people are falling into hell daily while we are going about our frivolous ways.

And lest you become overwhelmed by what you believe must be your response to such a statement, remember that one of the greatest things we can do to save souls is to *pray for them*. Another may be recorded as the one who helped lead them through the prayer of salvation, but God keeps excellent record books: if your prayers prepare a soul to set aside self in order to embrace spirit, I believe this is

---

* John 21:22

recorded in Heaven.* Equally, through our diverse callings, we endeavor to save many souls alive. So do not oppress your soul with more than what God is requiring of you. Just be diligent to fulfill the assignments the Lord has appointed you to complete.

Let those who want to keep their head buried in the sand declare it all conspiracy theory. If you want to know the truth, inquire of the Lord what is really going on. The truth will begin to seep in around you like the accumulation of heavy rain, but eventually you will be buoyed on waters too deep to stand in. And it will all be the truth you asked to know. Don't take my word for anything. Ask God, and then wait and

---

* I Corinthians 3:5-8—"Who then is Paul, and who is Apollos, but ministers by whom ye believed, even as the Lord gave to every man? I have planted, Apollos watered; but God gave the increase. So then neither is he that planteth any thing, neither he that watereth; but God that giveth the increase. Now he that planteth and he that watereth are one: and every man shall receive his own reward according to his own labour."

listen and be open to what is being said around you.

There is a tremendous amount of Kingdom work to finish before the end comes, even if that end does not occur for generations. Compare the time it seems we have left to demonstrate to this earth what the Body of Christ can really be, to the twenty centuries that have already passed without the Church ever having come fully into the New Testament paradigm for it. Even if we have a whole century left, even two, that is a mere tenth of what the Church failed to be as a corporate body these two thousand years. Do you want to waste it wrestling with God about what you believe ought to be, especially when He is not going to change Himself or His ways merely to suit your ideas of how the universe ought to be run? –and especially since He is accomplishing this great judgment to restore all that the enemy has stolen from the people? Don't throw it back into His face. If there is something that seems particularly harsh to you, take your burdens to Him. Resolve what needs to be resolved, but then get on board the Kingdom-train, my friend! Ride those swift-moving rails to whatever destination He has for us! For the blessing of the Lord exceeds anything we can contrive for ourselves. And trust the fate of Man to the One who created him.

If you can remember only one thing from all this, remember that it is God's right to deal with His creation as He wills and that His will *always* entails the best for us He can give according to how much the soul has surrendered to it and is willing to receive. If His wisdom determines that for a certain person death is the just sentence — and possibly the only sentence that will awaken this soul to the reality of what it faces, which is eternal death if it does

not repent and be reconciled to God —
then this is just. And if, in taking all
factors into account of degree of intent
to harm or ability to use in future as a
testimony of His grace, life imprisonment is the sentence He prefers to dole
out, or a much lesser sentence, it is for
Him to decide, not you. And this is
merely regarding the repentant. For the
unrepentant who have every intention
of continuing to conspire if they get any
chance at all to harm the little people
(even while completely justified that
we have been pretty stupid), no reprieve may be factored into His laws.
And even if there is no doubt that such
a soul is irrevocably set against God,
and He decides on imprisonment
rather than death, will you judge Him
for this? God knows that these are the
last years this soul will have before it
suffers in torment for all eternity. And
if He wishes to show the only mercy He
can within the boundaries of His Law
for Man, He may choose to do so.

Moreover, simply because a soul is tried by a human court and execution is enacted by human means, remember that when God's judgment becomes visible in this earth, His authority trumps all others. In such special times, no earthly authority is permitted to countermand what He has determined to accomplish, just as Pharaoh's will to destroy the Israelites meant nothing at the Red Sea because the LORD had determined this was the time to save His people according to His promise to Abraham. He *gave His word* that at the end of four centuries, He would bring Abraham's descendants back to the land of his sojourning. And so He kept His word. Yet what the people saw was Moses standing at the head of their company, rod stretched out over the water. But Moses declared that this was the LORD's doing.*

This letter is long, I realize, but there is another thing I wish to bring to

---

* Exodus 14:15-27

attention for your contemplation on this matter — not to overburden you with many meditations but to give you plenty to draw upon that might aid you in reconciling your questions.

Do you recall the designation of six sanctuary cities the LORD instructed Joshua to institute as the people began to occupy the land? Look at Joshua 20.*

I believe we are going to learn in time that many of those being judged in this historical hour are as those who sought sanctuary in a city of refuge but

---

* Examine also Numbers 35:9-34, which was the basis for Joshua's actions. As an interesting side note, consider that *20*, the chapter number, can be associated with the years of this century: these can be considered the 20s. Consider that God is reestablishing His standard for Man's behavior in this century, a standard that will not go overlooked or dispensed with as unnecessary throughout this era. And this standard is one that provides sanctuary under the Law for those who did not intentionally inflict harm. But such souls must still submit themselves to the parameters of this Law. For those who receive Jesus Christ as their Saviour, this is the New Law, the Blood-Covenant made with God through Him, and so we submit to the parameters of this Covenant, which declare there is but one standard for Man (a righteous one) and one means of salvation (Jesus Christ our Lord).

who did not meet the qualifications for living there. Unintentionally inflicted harm was the qualifier for being granted sanctuary in a city of refuge. And then even if found innocent of inflicting intentional harm on the one killed, the person still had to remain in that city for the rest of the current high priest's natural life — sort of serving a sentence in a kind of minimum-security prison: there were still geographical restrictions one could not pass beyond without risking retribution. So these boundaries were for the protection of the one acquitted of intentional harm from those who might avenge the killed person, but they also served as a consequence for what happened that could not be undone.

I believe we are going to learn that many, having in a sense made it to a sanctuary city, then bribed the legal system to make it appear that they committed no harm with conscious, deliberate attempt. But for this reason they are unqualified to remain within the boundaries of refuge, and the Law requires judgment—a life for a life. They would not receive the New Law of Christ, so this bounces them back to the old Law of retribution. *We* will have all manner of debt-forgiveness—which is an outer expression of the full forgiveness of our sins, our indebtedness to God—but they will be required to repay all that they were indebted to us for (which is basically what they stole from the people so that they could live high off of what should have remained with us), including the forfeiture of their life for the ones they took or deliberately purposed to take. We live under the New Law; they live under the old.

God has not established diverse systems by which our life is judged. A person can argue this his whole life, be proficient in the ways of countless philosophical systems, but argument will change nothing when he finds out at the Day of Judgment that this was the truth.

And I believe we are going to learn that many who found refuge within the confines of the old legal system, regardless that they corrupted this system to provide themselves with safety, were as those who conspired together to deprive the current high priest of the remainder of his natural life just so they would then be free to return to their old lives, wherever that might be outside the sanctuary city (and which without doubt included harm to their neighbors whenever they could profit by them in some way).

So if we judge God for being too harsh in His judgments, we are essentially condoning high crimes and murder for the purpose of circumventing His Law governing our behavior. We are declaring, whether we realize it or not, that people ought to escape just repercussions even for the crime of taking another's life. And many have taken many lives in their pursuit of power and wealth and a long life of personal liberty, and were far more directly involved in these deaths than I think most of us want to comprehend. (I.e., they did not just hire someone to do the deed but personally committed murder themselves.)

I do not consider myself a prophetic voice, only one who has an assignment to store up truth-seeds that may be scattered into the good soil of souls willing to come to a greater knowing of God. Yet God has raised up many such voices to issue warnings and to shed light on the world's current affairs and on God's Word as it applies to these days. I advise you to hear what some of them have to say, if you have not already. Test the spirit of their testimony. Do not accept what does not agree with the Word of God, as they ought to testify so themselves, but also give thoughtful consideration to those things that may seem to run counter to what you have been taught.

For we have all believed many lies across the generations of those now living, and we must all choose to awaken to truth or to continue to be in agreement with lies. As for me, I grew weary long ago of recognizing truths that most around me found it easy to disregard. Though few of us enjoy the separation that naturally occurs when we feel we cannot speak freely with those close to us, one gains the ability as time passes to continue on with God regardless of what occurs relationally with others or not. (And we do not speak freely because the soul who truly loves God gains a distaste for causing offense even to those who themselves do not seem to mind giving it.)

I feel for you, for I am not sure you have yet had the opportunity to gain the same. I would not wish all this to be hard for you. Our life questions are not put on us by God to make us miserable, but to give us opportunity to enter into greater reconciliation with Him. I wish you joy and gladness every day as you walk with God. But I know that the Path is not all sunshine and roses. The shadows can be long that are cast from the high fortresses of those who always seek to oppress the small ones.

Let us awaken to what God wants to do in this earth. Let us be faithful to test the spirits of things as instructed in His Word,* and let us come into agreement with whatever has the mark and tone of our Shepherd, who is good and who will not lead us astray. It is we who do not always hear rightly. He never misspeaks. There is judgment coming, but not for our destruction. It is for our preservation against those who are determined to destroy those allied with God, goodness, and truth.

Judgment is the removal of the old that cannot be of use in the new. All that is corrupt, foul, destructive, mean-

---

* I John 4:1

spirited, vindictive, murderous, etc., even frivolous if the spirit of frivolity interferes with His Holy Spirit moving among us, must be dealt with. (Childlike playfulness differs from a superficial atmosphere of frivolity.) These are all ancient forces that God prohibits in His Paradigm of the New — the full embodiment of the New Covenant of Christ at work in this earth.

It is not God's intent to wipe away every soul peripherally associated with these unclean forces. It is His intent to cleanse and reform. But He places boundaries on how long He will let these forces continue to be at work in this earth. And I believe we have reached that time. It is not the time of the very end: it is the time of *the example of the end,* that no soul will have excuse to declare later that it was not given the chance to know the truth of its existence as one created by a Sovereign God who required of it a choice of either for or against its Creator. Will this Great Reform eradicate evil in the earth forever? No. We can read in His Word that when enough time has passed, it will rally and rise again—twice more: once during and around the time known as the Tribulation, and once at the end of the Millennial era. At this time evil's *strongholds* are being demolished—those spiritual infrastructures that enabled it to work so effectively in this earth across the great peaks of influence. The Black Death will pass away, but not every rat will cease to exist. But they will scurry for their dark holes; the sun will shine again; and we will breathe cleaner air than we ever have before. Those who would willingly occupy the high fortresses will still exist (though not in such great profusion); yet their ability to refashion such fortresses will be demolished as these infrastructures come down.

So it is the organized foundation of evil, that well-oiled machinery engineered to accomplish thievery and destruction, that God is destroying in this time. He has not and does not intend to destroy all those stupid people who have without under-standing built their life on this foundation. It is those who were aware of the forces they were harnessing against their fellow souls and who refused to repent of this that will fall under His judgment. If any die who do not seem to be guilty of such an association, do not burden yourself with too many questions for too long. Perhaps God is bringing many Home because He knows that is where they would prefer to be, or because He is altering the spiritual landscape know-ing many influential teachers will not know how to transition from what they taught for decades to what we must become. We shall see.

Look at it this way: the great skyscraper of the world's systems has become worthy of condemnation. Its structure has become unsteady, its wiring a fire hazard, its plumbing ready to burst and the force of this bursting bring the unsteady structure crumbling to the ground. Would you recommend adding onto the building under such conditions, or would you advise tearing it down and starting new?

God wants to tear down the old world system and build a new structure. That someday evil will succeed to some extent in rebuilding it—well, are you saying it is futile to labor now for the Kingdom until God catches up His Church and leaves this world with its evil? How many souls could be saved during this time that will pass into Heaven, safe forever from hell and evil? A billion-soul harvest has been prophesied! And I declare one billion is not enough, Lord! Give us two billion, even three! Give Thy Son the nations of this world for the glory of Thy Name and Thy Kingdom!*

Should we not finish the work God has assigned for His Church — finish the ministry of His Son, who is the Head to our Body? In order to do this, this earth must be cleansed. The bowls are full, and the earth cries out for redemption and reformation. Our God will *not* turn a deaf ear to the poor, oppressed peoples across this earth. He hears their cries, and it is time to come rescue them.

We have had access to bits of the new our whole lives, but the overall *system* in which we have lived has not been of God's design. We have strived to fit those bits into a super-system that was designed to leave God out of our life-equations. This is why it has failed to provide us with workable solutions on so many accounts.

---

* Psalm 2:8—"Ask of Me, and I shall give Thee the heathen for Thine inheritance, and the uttermost parts of the earth for Thy possession."

(And make no mistake, it is a single world system. People declare against a One World Government as though this has not yet occurred. But I tell you, there has already been one in existence to a great extent. The fight of late has been the battle to have we the people openly acknowledge the lordship of a few so that these few could more freely rule over us. But a worldwide system of thievery, destruction, and oppression is no new occurrence. The One World Government successfully in place at the time of the end will be one that will incorporate all facets of society—government, religion, business, etc. Presently the shiny distraction of personal choice—mostly contrived, I might add, for our choices are relentlessly herded toward destructive ends through many subtle and cunning methods—has been left so that the enemy could infiltrate areas of our existence while our gaze was elsewhere.)

The old has been judged. It has been placed on the LORD's scales and found wanting in goodness, justice, mercy — in any real virtue at all.*

God will not remove His Church from this earth without illustrating that every attempt had been made to awaken the people to the reality that there is One True God and One Saviour of mankind. I believe this is the time in which judgment is being illustrated. And along with judgment, deliverance, promotion, blessing, fulfillment, and everything positive the Lord intended on bringing into this earth by the creation of His Church.

So do not lose heart. If you become fearful, angry, or overwhelmed by what is occurring, run to your prayer cell and shut its door fast. Sequester yourself for a time away from the noise and apparent chaos, and let the world tumble down around you. Since you

---

* Daniel 5:27

are not of the world,* since you are hid in Christ with God,† it cannot touch you—at least it cannot where it really counts. Leave everything you do not understand with God when you depart that little room. Shelve it, and walk away. And let us continue to surrender ourselves to His judgment—trusting that for those who bear the new stain of His Son's Blood, He will pour out mercy upon us. These are weighty times and weighty matters. Take your rest as often as you feel strained in your soul. God will remain Sovereign in the meanwhile.

So let us be faithful to God, and let Him be what He will be. He will be the Most High Judge, and we His devoted and faithful followers who may not understand everything He does but who trust Him implicitly to make just decrees.

---

* John 17:16
† Colossians 3:3

And when we see things happening that tempt us to exercise a judgmental attitude toward Him, let us shut our eyes fast to what is happening in the world — however just it might be — and run to our prayer cell and plead Jesus to show us again how God is Love.

Remind yourself again that there is lovely land on the mountain of feeling, but it is not the best place to build a home. Like the multitude of variety in the mountain regions of our great states, there is no lack of vistas for recreational activities. But for everyday living, life on the mountain of feeling is harder than life on the mountain of faith. It is like living in the Appalachian Mountains in comparison with the Rocky Mountains, which possess numerous differences. The acreage on the mountain of faith is rich and suitable for the sowing of many and varied plants with the expectation of bountiful harvests. The soul firmly established in God vacations now and again on the mountain of feeling, those western mountains where there are many recreational things that can be done with others during those short periods of escape from the everyday. But it *lives* on the mountain of faith where it counts on the seasonal sowing and reaping for which the climate is better suited. Live on the mountain of faith. If you have lost your way during a visit to the mountain of feeling, retrace your path to the mountain of faith and reenter the everyday course of living with God. This will help you immensely, as I hope this letter has also helped you in some small way.

Let us pray together — *May the God of all grace transform many tares into wheat as He did water into wine and sinners into saints, to save unto everlasting life those who would otherwise be lost forever. In Jesus' Name, God help us all.*

The grace of our Lord Jesus Christ, the love of the Father, and the fellowship of the Holy Spirit be with you always. Amen.

www.ingramcontent.com/pod-product-compliance
Lightning Source LLC
Chambersburg PA
CBHW021339160726
47994CB00007B/2765